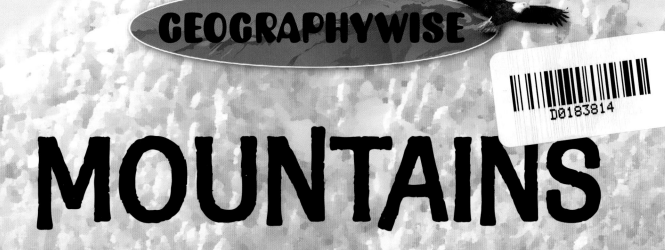

GEOGRAPHYWISE

MOUNTAINS

Jen Green

WAYLAND

Published in paperback in 2014 by Wayland

Copyright © Wayland 2014

Wayland
Hachette Children's Books
338 Euston Road
London NW1 3BH

Wayland Australia
Level 17/207 Kent Street
Sydney, NSW 2000

Editorial Director: Rasha Elsaeed
Editor: Katie Powell
Designer: Tim Mayer, Mayer Media
Illustrator: Peter Bull Art Studio
Consultant: Meg Gillett

British Library Cataloguing in Publication Data

Green, Jen.
  Geographywise.
  Mountains.
  1. Mountains--Juvenile literature.
  I. Title
  910'.02143-dc22

ISBN 9780750286770

Printed in Malaysia

10 9 8 7 6 5 4 3 2 1

Wayland is a division of Hachette Children's Books,
an Hachette UK company.

Picture acknowledgements
Title page © Istock (repeat p 21b), imprint and contents
page © Istock (repeat p5b), P4(b) © Istock, p5(br)
© Istock, p4-5 © Wayland, P6-7 © Wayland, P7 ©
Shutterstock, P8(t) and cover © Istock, P8(b) © Wayland,
P9 © Anup Shah/Naturepl.com, P10 © Wayland,
P11 © Time & Life Pictures/Getty Images, P12 ©
Shutterstock, P12-13 © Istock, P14 (t&b) © Wayland,
P15, 16 © Istock, P17,18 © Wayland, P19 (t,c left,b) ©
Istock, P19 (c right) Shutterstock, P20 © Istock, P21(t) ©
Istock, P21(b) © Istock (repeat p1), P22(t) 42-20895685
© Jacques Ducoin/Sygma/Corbis, P22 © Shutterstock,
P22-23 © Istock, P23(t) ABJXAR © Alamy/ Matthew
Totton, P24 © Shutterstock, P25 0000212991-005 ©
Jacques Langevin/Sygma/Corbis, P26 © Shutterstock,
P27 © Istock, P28 © Wayland, P29 © Istock, P30,31,32 ©
Istock (repeat p5b)

Contents

What are mountains?

A mountain is a steep-sided mass of rock that stands above the landscape. High ground above 500 metres is generally called a mountain. Hills are lower than 500 metres. Some mountains stand alone, but most are found in groups called **ranges**. A long mountain range is called a chain.

Mountains have dramatic scenery, such as cliffs, **crags** and glittering lakes. The highest point is called the peak or **summit**.

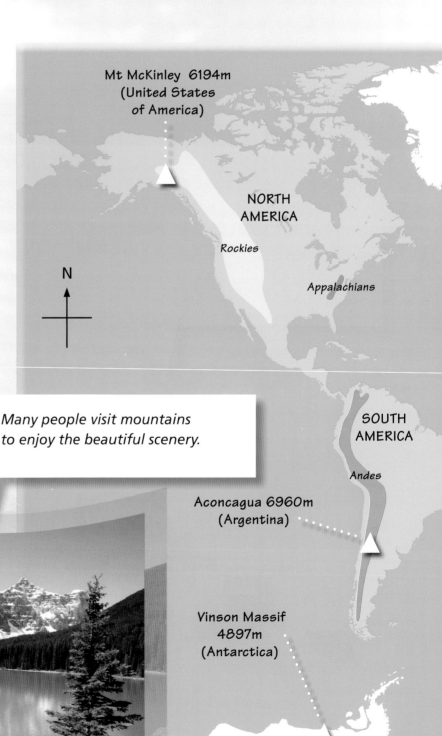

Mt McKinley 6194m
(United States
of America)

NORTH
AMERICA

Rockies

Appalachians

N

SOUTH
AMERICA

Andes

Aconcagua 6960m
(Argentina)

Vinson Massif
4897m
(Antarctica)

ANTARCTICA

Many people visit mountains to enjoy the beautiful scenery.

The higher you climb on a mountain, the colder it gets. This is because cool air rises. Many high mountains are covered with ice and snow all year round. Some plants and animals can live on mountains, despite the cold conditions.

People live there, too. This book will explain how mountains form and how plants, animals and people live on mountains.

Elbrus 5633m
(Russia)

Mt Blanc 4810m
(Italy/France)

ASIA

Urals

EUROPE

Mt Everest 8848m
(Nepal/Tibet)

Alps

Himalayas

Atlas Mountains

AFRICA

Ethiopian
Highlands

East African
Mountains

Mt Kilimanjaro
5,895m
(Tanzania)

AUSTRALASIA

Great
Dividing
Range

Mt Kosciuszko
2228m
(Australia)

The Himalayas in Asia are the highest mountain range. They include Mount Everest, the world's highest mountain at 8,848 metres. The longest mountain chain is the Andes in South America at 7,200 kilometres long.

This map shows the world's greatest mountain ranges. There are mountains in every part of the world.

Some people also visit mountains to hike, climb or ski.

5

Fold mountains

Mountains are formed by incredibly powerful forces. Below Earth's surface is a thick layer of red-hot rocks called the **mantle**. These rocks are so hot they melt and flow very slowly, like thick treacle.

Earth's outer layer, called the **crust**, is made of giant rocky slabs called **plates**. These fit together like a cracked eggshell. Currents of hot rock flowing in the mantle cause the plates to drift slowly across Earth's surface. They may scrape past one another, crash together or drift apart.

Crust

Mantle

Outer core

Inner core

Beneath the hard, cold, rock surface, the inside of the Earth is red hot.

This map shows the plates that form Earth's surface. They fit together like a huge jigsaw.

Where two plates collide, the border zone crumples upward to form a range of **fold mountains**. The Himalayas, the Rocky Mountains in North America and the Alps in Europe all formed in this way.

MOUNT EVEREST

By 1900, Mount Everest was recognised as the world's highest mountain. Many mountaineers tried to climb it, but failed. Then in 1953, two members of a British team, Edmund Hillary and Tenzing Norgay, managed to reach the top.

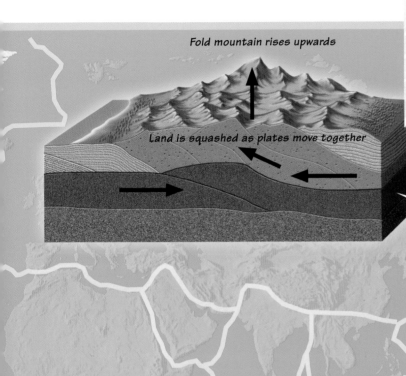

Fold mountain rises upwards

Land is squashed as plates move together

This diagram shows how fold mountains form. When squeezed, rocks form folds rather like the folds you can make by squashing up a tablecloth.

These mountains in Alberta, Canada, were formed by folding.

Block mountains and rift valleys

Mountains form in other ways besides folding, too. Plate movements put rocks under enormous strain. Eventually they shatter to form deep cracks called **faults**. Most faults are found along the borders of plates. Sometimes the rocks can stick for a time but then suddenly jolt into a new position. The violent jolt is an **earthquake**.

Mount Rundle in the Rocky Mountains of Canada is a block mountain.

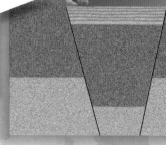

*This diagram shows how a **block mountain** and a **rift valley** form.*

Block of land slides down between faults to form a rift valley

Block of land is squeezed upwards to make a block mountain

Where plates press together, a slab of rock between two faults may be forced upwards. The higher land is called a block mountain. The Teton Range in Wyoming, USA and the Harz Mountains in Germany are block mountains.

Where plates drift apart, the cracks along faults get wider. A block of land between two faults can drop downwards. The result is a deep, flat-bottomed valley called a rift valley. The Great Rift Valley in East Africa is an example of this.

UNBELIEVABLE!

The Great Rift Valley stretches for around 6,000 kilometres. It runs from East Africa all the way to Syria in southwest Asia. The Red Sea and the Dead Sea both lie in the bed of this huge valley.

This picture shows the Great Rift Valley. Some of Africa's highest mountains are on the edge of the valley, which is 160 kilometres wide.

Volcanoes

Many mountain peaks that stand alone are volcanoes. A **volcano** forms where red-hot rock from deep underground surges up and explodes onto the surface. This is called an **eruption**. Streams of hot rock called **lava** erupt from the volcano. Ash, gas and steam shoot into the air.

.... Cloud of ash

...... Opening (vent)

Lava . . . .

Main pipe

Cone formed of layers of ash and lava

Side pipe . . . . . .

Red-hot rock collects in a hollow chamber

This diagram shows what happens when a volcano erupts.

Over time lava cools and hardens to form solid rock. If the eruptions are repeated, ash and lava build up to form a mountain. Some volcanoes erupt thick, sticky lava which hardens quickly to form a tall, cone-shaped mountain. Other volcanoes ooze runny lava which flows further before cooling, and a more rounded volcano forms. Erupting volcanoes are very dangerous. In 1902, a volcano called Mount Pelée erupted on the Caribbean island of Martinique. Burning ash and lava rained down on the nearby town of St Pierre, and 38,000 people died.

THE END OF POMPEII

In AD 79, a volcano called Vesuvius erupted in Italy. Burning ash buried the Roman town of Pompeii. The Roman writer Pliny watched the eruption. He described a huge black cloud of ash, shaped like a pine tree, rising from the mountain.

In 1980, Mount St Helens in western United States erupted violently. Clouds of ash blasted high into the air. The explosion blew off the mountain's top.

Wearing away

Mountains are often high and jagged as a result of extreme weathering. Over time, they get lower and more rounded. This happens as the rocks at the surface **erode**, or wear away. Ice, wind and water erode bits of rock and carry them away.

Rocks heat up in the Sun by day, and cool at night. This constant heating and cooling makes rocks crack. Water seeps into the cracks and freezes at night to form ice. Ice makes the rocks split. Pieces break off and are swept away by wind or water, or tumble downhill.

*Shattered fragments of rocks pile up at the foot of slopes. This debris is called **scree**.*

GRAND CANYON

The Grand Canyon is one of the world's deepest gorges, 1.6 kilometres deep. In 1869, John Wesley Powell led an expedition which explored the canyon by boat. Powell was a rock expert and ex-soldier who had lost an arm in battle.

Fast-flowing streams erode narrow, V-shaped valleys in hills and mountains. Further downstream, small rivers called **tributaries** join to make even bigger rivers. These powerful rivers cut vertically into the rock, forming steep-sided **gorges** and **canyons**. The Grand Canyon in western USA is an example.

*The Grand Canyon formed where the Colorado River cut down through a high **plateau**. Flat-topped mountains rear high above the river bed.*

Carved by ice

Snow Peak ......

Much of the amazing scenery you find in mountains has been eroded by **glaciers**. Glaciers are huge masses of ice which form in high mountains. Glaciers move very slowly downhill. They act like giant bulldozers, carving away the sides of narrow valleys to form deep **troughs**.

Where ice collects between mountain peaks it erodes a bowl-shaped hollow. Later, if this fills with rain water, it forms a small, round lake called a **tarn**. Where glaciers erode a mountain from all sides, they can carve a steep-sided peak called a **pyramidal peak**.

Pyramidal Peak ......

Tarn ......

This diagram shows how glaciers carve deep, flat-bottomed valleys, tarns and pyramidal peaks.

BURIED BODY

In 1991, two climbers found a man's body in a glacier in the Alps. Scientists discovered that the man had died 5,000 years ago! The ice had preserved his body. He was a hunter who probably died in a blizzard when crossing the mountains.

Thousands of years ago, the weather was colder than it is now. This time is called an **Ice Age**. Ice and snow covered much of Europe and North America. Glaciers left U-shaped valleys, pyramidal peaks and **tarns** in places that are free of ice today.

As the ice in a glacier moves downhill it gouges a deep valley. Stones dragged along the bottom scrape away more rock.

Mountain weather

Temperatures on mountains are colder than land at lower altitudes. Because of the cold, snow falls instead of rain, and high peaks remain snow-covered even in summer. Spring arrives late and autumn comes early. This means that mountains have short summers and long, icy winters.

Hikers have to be ready for all kinds of weather in the mountains.

Mountains are also windy places because there is no higher land around to provide shelter. Strong winds bring quickly-changing weather. One moment it may be warm and sunny, then storm clouds appear, or a cold mist creeps over the mountains. A strong wind makes the air feel colder, too.

Mountains have unusual rainfall patterns. Mountain slopes facing the wind are usually the wettest. When warm, moist air hits the mountain, it rises and cools. Clouds form and rain falls. The air has no moisture left when it reaches the far side of the mountain, so this part is very dry. This is called the **rain shadow** effect.

UNBELIEVABLE!

High mountains such as the Himalayas produce extreme rainfall patterns. Southern slopes of these mountains lie in the path of wet winds. This is one of the wettest places on Earth. But the mountains create a rain shadow. On the north side is a vast desert.

Where moist winds blow toward a mountain, most rain falls on the nearest slope. The far side, called the rain shadow, gets very little rain.

Clouds and rain

Moist air

Rain shadow

Mountain wildlife

Plants and animals that live on mountains have to be tough to cope with the harsh, wintry weather. Plants and even trees grow close to the ground to shelter from icy winds. Some plants have hairy leaves or stems to keep out the cold.

As you climb a mountain, the air temperature falls. The **vegetation** changes, too. Trees grow on lower slopes, but fade out at a point called the **tree line**. Grassy meadows are found higher up, but higher still there is only bare rock, often covered with ice and snow.

This diagram shows the vegetation that grows at different heights on mountains.

Snow-covered peak

Bare rock

Grassy slope

Tree line

Forests on lower slopes

Mountain animals usually have thick fur or feathers. Goats and sheep are shaggy animals with rubbery hooves that can grip rock. They move up the mountain to feed in summer. But in winter they migrate down to shelter in forests on the lower slopes.

Marmot

Pika

*Marmots spend more than six months of the year in a deep sleep called **hibernation**.*

UNBELIEVABLE!

Marmots and pikas are two types of burrowing mammals that survive high on mountains. Marmots spend the long, bitterly cold winter months hibernating in their burrows. Pikas have a different tactic. They gather grass in autumn to provide food and warm bedding in winter. Thanks to a ready supply of food and bedding, they do not need to hibernate.

The yak is a huge shaggy creature with the longest hair of any animal. It lives high in the Himalayas.

Living in the mountains

Mountains are home to fewer people than lowland areas because of the harsh conditions. Even so, some people have lived in mountain regions for centuries. There are villages, towns and even cities. However, people settle in the valleys, not on the summits, because valleys offer shelter, water and flatter land.

Steep slopes and harsh weather make travel difficult. Roads and railways keep to valleys wherever possible. Roads zigzag up high passes to cross mountain ranges. Special railways climb steep slopes. Cable cars, ski-lifts, skis, planes and helicopters all help people get about.

Lhasa, in Tibet, is the world's highest city. It lies at 3,660 metres, high up in the Himalayas.

Ski-tourism is an industry in many mountain regions.

*This village in the Alps is a **resort**. It provides work for local people who run hotels or act as guides.*

Nowadays mountains attract large numbers of visitors. Tourists come to ski in winter, and hike, climb or go biking in summer. Villages called resorts have been built just for tourists. New roads, railways and airports help people reach these resorts.

UNBELIEVABLE!

La Paz in Bolivia is the world's highest capital city. It stands at 3,632 metres in the Andes Mountains. At this height the air contains less oxygen. People who reach La Paz by plane sometimes get a headache because they aren't used to the thin mountain air.

Working in the mountains

The people who live and work in mountain areas earn a living in different ways. Some work as farmers. Steps called **terraces** are cut into steep slopes to make flat land for farming. Sheep, goats and cattle graze on land that is too steep to grow crops during the summer months.

*In winter, farmers take their animals down from the steep mountain slopes to farms in order to shelter them from the cold and snow. This is called **transhumance**.*

Two villagers returning home with a stack of wood for burning. In some mountain regions, a lot of the forests have been cut down for fuel.

Villagers have cut steps into this mountain's steep sides so they can work and farm on the land around their homes.

STRIKING GOLD!

In the 1890s, gold was discovered in the Klondike, part of the Rocky Mountains in northern Canada. People flocked to this remote, icy region in the hope of finding gold. Many miners died of cold on the long journey. Very few struck gold and became rich.

This miner in a silver mine in the Andes is preparing to blast away the rock to reach the silver, using a small explosion.

Mining is often important. Gold, silver, copper, tin and diamonds are mined in some mountain ranges. Granite and slate are quarried for building. Some people work as loggers, cutting down forests for timber and fuel.

The energy of fast-flowing mountain streams can be used to produce electricity. This is called **hydroelectric power**. A dam is built to control the flow of water, and a reservoir forms behind it. These reservoirs often provide water for nearby towns, as well as recreation areas for local people.

Mountain dangers

A huge mass of snow crashes downhill in an avalanche.

Mountains can be dangerous, both for visitors and local people. Climbers, hikers and skiers can get lost in mist or blizzards. People can die of cold if they are injured and can't reach safety. Luckily, rescue teams are on hand to help lost or injured people.

Landslides and **avalanches** are a danger on steep slopes. A landslide strikes when rock and soil break loose and crash down the mountain. An avalanche happens when a mass of snow sweeps downhill. Landslides and avalanches can carry away roads, trees and even towns.

Some people choose to settle on the slopes of volcanoes because the soil is good for farming. However, if the volcano erupts many people can die. In 1985, a volcano called Nevado del Ruiz erupted in the Andes. Burning ash mixed with snow to form a tide of mud, which buried the town of Armero. Around 23,000 people died.

LOST IN A CREVASSE

In 1985, British climber Joe Simpson broke a leg while climbing in the Andes. His partner tried to lower him on a rope, but Simpson ended up in a crevasse with a broken rope. Somehow he managed to crawl out of the crevasse and down the mountain to safety.

*Heavy rain in the mountains can cause a sudden flood which sweeps away roads and houses. This is called a **flash flood**.*

Taking care of mountains

Mountains look tough and solid but, in fact, they can easily be damaged. Mining and logging can damage mountains by speeding up erosion. Miners strip away grass, soil and rock to reach valuable minerals. Loggers cut down trees whose roots help to keep the soil together. When trees and grass have been removed, heavy rain can wash the soil away.

Large numbers of tourists may also damage mountains. People may drop litter, pick flowers or frighten wildlife. Cars, trains and planes that bring tourists cause **pollution**. People's feet and skis trample on the earth and this can erode the soil.

Tourists have dropped a large amount of litter in the Himalayan mountains over the years.

The autumn scenery in Yellowstone National Park is beautiful to see.

People are now learning to take better care of mountains. Erosion can be reduced by controlling logging and mining. National parks and nature reserves have been set up to protect mountains and their wildlife. Here no one is allowed to pick plants or harm animals. The motto of such parks is: 'Take nothing but photos; leave nothing but footprints.'

UNBELIEVABLE!

In 1872, the world's first national park was set up in Yellowstone, high in the Rocky Mountains, USA. Now national parks protect beautiful mountains the world over. Sagamartha National Park in the Himalayas protects the area around Everest. The park authorities organise clean-ups to remove litter.

Explore a mountain!

Maps of mountains

Look at a map of a mountain region. What does it tell you about the landscape? Mountains are shown on maps using lines called **contour lines**. When the lines are close together, the slope is steep. Can you see lakes, rivers and forests?

Look for roads, towns and villages. Where are they located? Why do you think they have been built in these locations? Does the map show things to do if you visit the mountains?

This map shows a mountain called Helvellyn in the Lake District, England. Several paths lead to the summit.

HELVELLYN

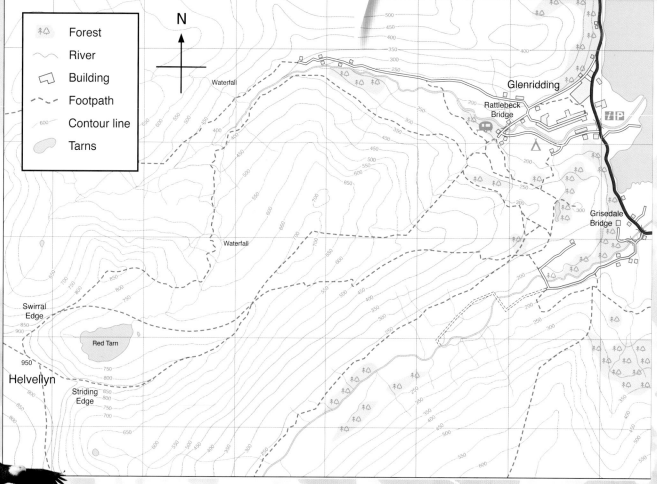

Legend:
- 🌲 Forest
- River
- Building
- Footpath
- Contour line
- Tarns

N

Waterfall
Glenridding
Rattlebeck Bridge
600
Waterfall
Swirral Edge
850
900
Red Tarn
950
Helvellyn
Striding Edge
Grisedale Bridge

Visit a mountain

Take a trip to the mountains. Whether you travel by road or rail, you will probably arrive in a valley. What is the weather like? Look at the landscape from the valley. What sort of farming happens along the valley bottom? Can you see plants and animals that are different from the ones at home?

Now set off up the mountain, either on foot or by road, train or cable car. Is the weather different at the top? Can you see any snow? What sort of farming goes on here? Are the plants and animals here different to the ones in the valley?

The scenery and conditions on a mountain-top are very different to those in the valley below.

Warning! *Always tell an adult where you are going before you go for your mountain walk.*

29

Cross-curricular links

Use this topic web to investigate mountains in other parts of your curriculum.

English & Literacy
Find out about a particular volcanic eruption or deadly avalanche using your local library or the Internet. Write about the disaster as if you had been there.

Citizenship
Find out more about threats to mountain wildlife. Make a poster explaining how everyone can help protect wildlife in the mountains.

MOUNTAINS

History
Use the Internet or library books to find out about a town in a mountain area. When and why did the town grow up? What work do people do there? Is tourism important?

Science
Use a library or the Internet to find out more about the feeding habits of mountain animals. Do they eat plants or other animals? Can you draw a food web showing the links between the plants and animals?

Design and Technology
Draw a map of your favourite mountain range in the middle of a large piece of paper. Draw pictures or take photos of mountain scenery, plants and animals, and stick them around the edge.

Glossary

Avalanche When a mass of snow and rock slides down a mountain.

Block mountain A mountain formed when a block of land is forced up between two faults.

Canyon A deep, steep-sided valley.

Contour lines Lines on a map which show the height above sea level.

Crag A steep rock face.

Crust Earth's outer layer.

Earthquake When the ground shakes as rocks move deep underground.

Erosion When rock or soil are worn away and carried off by wind, ice or flowing water.

Erupt When a volcano gives off ash, gas, steam or lava.

Fault A deep crack in the rocks of Earth's surface.

Flash flood A serious flood that occurs quickly and without warning.

Fold mountain A mountain that forms when land crumples up between two plates.

Glacier A mass of ice that moves downhill.

Gorge A deep valley with steep sides.

Hibernation A deep sleep that allows animals to survive winter.

Hydroelectric power Electricity that is produced using fast-flowing water.

Ice Age A long, cold period in Earth's history, when ice covered much of the land.

Landslide When a mass of rock and soil falls downhill.

Lava Hot, melted rock from a volcano.

Mantle A layer of red-hot rock beneath Earth's surface.

Plate One of the giant rocky slabs that make up the Earth's crust.

Plateau A flat-topped mountain.

Pollution When the air, water or soil is harmed.

Pyramidal peak A sharp mountain summit formed by ice erosion.

Rain shadow An area that is dry because a mountain shields it from moist winds.

Range A group of mountains.

Resort A place where people go on holiday.

Rift valley A valley formed when a block of land drops down between two faults.

Scree Fragments of rock that have tumbled down the mountain.

Summit The mountain top.

Tarn A small mountain lake.

Terrace A step cut into a hillside to make a field.

Transhumance The moving of animals.

Tree line The place on a mountain beyond which trees cannot grow.

Tributary A smaller river or stream that joins a larger river.

Trough Narrow valleys carved away by glaciers.

Vegetation The plants that grow in an area.

Volcano An opening which allows hot, melted rock and ash to escape during an eruption.

Index

Further information

Books

Mountains Around the World (Geography Now) by Jen Green, Wayland, 2008

Mountains (Geography Detective Investigates) by Jen Green, Wayland, 2009

Mountains (Geography Fact Files) by Anna Claybourne, Wayland, 2007

Websites

Learning about mountains: http://www.mountain.org/education/

Facts about mountains and volcanoes: http://www.woodlands-junior.kent.sch.uk/Homework/mountains/volcanoes.htm

Facts about mountains and interviews with people who live in mountains all over the world: http://www.mountainvoices.org/

National Parks in the UK: http://www.nationalparks.gov.uk/